A ROOKIE READER

HI, CLOUDS

By Carol Greene

Illustrations by Gene Sharp

Prepared under the direction of Robert Hillerich, Ph.D.

CHILDRENS PRESS ™

CHICAGO

This book is for Rachel.

Library of Congress Cataloging in Publication Data

Greene, Carol.
  Hi, clouds.

  (Rookie reader)
  Includes index.
  Summary: Two children watch clouds become fat and
thin, white and gray, then turn into dogs, sheep,
dragons, and castles.
  [1. Clouds—Fiction]   I. Title.   II. Series.
PZ7.G82845Hg   1983   [E]   82-19854
ISBN 0-516-02036-6

19 20 21 R 02 01 00 99 98

Hi, clouds.

3

Hi, fat cloud.

Hi, thin cloud.

Hi, white cloud.

Hi, gray cloud.

Oh, oh.

Don't rain, cloud.

Look! A cloud dog.

A cloud fish.

A cloud frog.

Oh! A cloud sheep.

15

Many sheep…

asleep.

Wow!

A cloud dragon.

A cloud covered wagon.

Cloud castle.

Cloud tree.

Cloud you.

Cloud me.

Oh, oh. Cloud clock.

Bye, clouds!

30

WORD LIST

a	dragon	oh
asleep	fat	rain
bye	fish	sheep
castle	frog	thin
clock	gray	tree
cloud(s)	hi	wagon
covered	look	white
dog	many	wow
don't	me	you

About the Author

Carol Greene has written over 25 books for children, plus stories, poems, songs, and filmstrips. She has also worked as a children's editor and a teacher of writing for children. She received a B.A. in English Literature from Park College, Parkville, Missouri, and an M.A. in Musicology from Indiana University. Ms. Greene lives in St. Louis, Missouri. When she isn't writing, she likes to read, travel, sing, do volunteer work at her church — and write some more. Her *The Super Snoops and the Missing Sleepers, Sandra Day O'Connor, First Woman on the Supreme Court,* and *Holidays Around the World* (a new true book) have also been published by Childrens Press.

About the Artist

Gene Sharp has illustrated several books in the Rookie Reader series including *Too Many Balloons* and *Please, Wind?* He would like to dedicate the pictures in this book to Laura who loves pictures and Alan who is learning to also love the words.